797,885 Books
are available to read at

Forgotten Books

www.ForgottenBooks.com

Forgotten Books' App
Available for mobile, tablet & eReader

ISBN 978-1-331-19473-6
PIBN 10156814

This book is a reproduction of an important historical work. Forgotten Books uses state-of-the-art technology to digitally reconstruct the work, preserving the original format whilst repairing imperfections present in the aged copy. In rare cases, an imperfection in the original, such as a blemish or missing page, may be replicated in our edition. We do, however, repair the vast majority of imperfections successfully; any imperfections that remain are intentionally left to preserve the state of such historical works.

Forgotten Books is a registered trademark of FB &c Ltd.
Copyright © 2015 FB &c Ltd.
FB &c Ltd, Dalton House, 60 Windsor Avenue, London, SW19 2RR.
Company number 08720141. Registered in England and Wales.

For support please visit www.forgottenbooks.com

1 MONTH OF FREE READING

at

www.ForgottenBooks.com

By purchasing this book you are eligible for one month membership to ForgottenBooks.com, giving you unlimited access to our entire collection of over 700,000 titles via our web site and mobile apps.

To claim your free month visit:

www.forgottenbooks.com/free156814

* Offer is valid for 45 days from date of purchase. Terms and conditions apply.

Similar Books Are Available from
www.forgottenbooks.com

The History of Napoleon Bonaparte
by R. H. Horne

England's Battles By Sea and Land
A Complete Record, by Unknown Author

Frederick the Great and the Rise of Prussia
by W. F. Reddaway

The German Air Force in the Great War
by J. E. Gurdon

The Battle of Groton Heights
by John J. Copp

Battlefields of the World War, Western and Southern Fronts
A Study in Military Geography, by Douglas Wilson Johnson

Battles of Chattanooga, Fought Nov. 23-25, 1863, by the Armies of the Cumberland and Tennessee
by William Wehner

The Campaign of Waterloo
A Military History, by John Codman Ropes

Cawnpore
by George Trevelyan

Famous Modern Battles
by A. Hilliard Atteridge

The Fifteen Decisive Battles, of the World, from Marathon to Waterloo
by Sir Edward Creasy

Germany and the Next War
by Friedrich von Bernhardi

The History of Hyder Shah, Alias Hyder Ali Khan Bahadur, and of His Son, Tippoo Sultaun
by M. M. D. L. T.

The History of the Thirty Years' War in Germany
Translated from the German, by Frederick Schiller

History of the War in Afghanistan, Vol. 1 of 3
by John William Kaye

History of the World War
With Chronology of Important Events, by Thomas R. Best

Naval Warfare
Its Ruling Principles and Practice Historically Treated, by P. H. Colomb

Records of the Revolutionary War
by William Thomas Saffell

Why Italy Entered Into the Great War
by Luigi Carnovale

1812; The War, and Its Moral
A Canadian Chronicle, by William F. Coffin

A TRUE ACCOUNT OF THE
BATTLE OF JUTLAND

MAY 31, 1916

By
THOMAS G. FROTHINGHAM
CAPTAIN, U. S. R.

Author of
*A Guide to the Military History of
The World War
1914-1918*

CAMBRIDGE, MASSACHUSETTS
BACON & BROWN
1920

Copyright, Bacon & Brown

PREFACE

THE following is an account of the essential facts of the Battle of Jutland, amplified from the review in the author's book, *A Guide to the Military History of The World War, 1914–1918*, published this year by Little, Brown & Co. This gives a greatly needed description of the events of the naval action, with the forces of both sides placed in true relation, one to the other.

No previously published account had contained an adequate treatment of the manœuvres of both fleets, as certain important events of the action were not understood, and it had been assumed that situations existed for which there was no foundation in fact. All this has resulted in a mass of confused and erroneous narratives — and the Battle of Jutland has become one of the most misunderstood actions in history.

The British Admiralty has announced that an official record of the Battle of Jutland would not be given out. Instead of this, the official dispatches covering the action have been issued in the form of a Blue-book. The publication of these documents does not help to solve many vexed questions — and the need is all the more evident of a trustworthy account of the action.

The reader may feel sure that the real course of the great naval battle has been traced in the present version, and that the facts here given have been established beyond dispute. In this way a reliable basis has been provided for reading narratives of the action, for studying the details of its varying fortunes — and for correcting many erroneous impressions which have been current.

A portion of the text was published in the Boston Evening *Transcript* of October 9, 1920. Two of the charts have been reproduced from *A Guide to the Military History of The World War*, and the thanks of the author are given to Messrs. Little, Brown & Co. for their courtesy in allowing use of the text of the book.

LIST OF TABLES

Table I.   The British Grand Fleet at the Battle of Jutland   6

Table II.   The German High Seas Fleet at the Battle of Jutland   7

LIST OF CHARTS

Chart showing the Battle of Jutland, in relation to the surroundings on the North Sea   9

Chart No. 1.   Typical British Chart, of the later manœuvres of the action which are in dispute   31

Chart No. 2.   The Battle of Jutland . . facing   54
        Chart No. 2 is so placed that it can be opened outside the pages for use as the text is being read.

THE BATTLE OF JUTLAND
MAY 31, 1916

Authorities quoted in the text are indicated as follows: Admiral Jellicoe (J), Vice Admiral Beatty (B), Admiral Scheer (S).

THE Battle of Jutland has been made a matter of bitter controversy, and accounts of the action have been so molded to fit partisan theories that the actual events have become obscured. Yet these events can now be determined through means that were never before available in the case of a great naval battle. Both commanders have published their detailed accounts, and there is no longer any reason for uncertainty as to the essentials of the action. Many of the tales from Germany were obviously untrue, but Admiral Scheer, the German Commander-in-Chief, has given a straightforward story of the battle which supplements the version of Admiral Jellicoe, the British Commander-in-Chief.

When the wide field of operations is taken into account, the two narratives of the rival commanders agree to a surprising extent as to the events of the early stages of the action. The engagement between the two advanced forces, the advent of the German High Seas Fleet, and the running fight

2 THE BATTLE OF JUTLAND

to meet the British Grand Fleet, are related in confirmation of Lord Jellicoe's report, and of the account in his book. Concerning the events of these first phases of the battle the various British narratives also practically agree.

Most of the differences and controversies relate to the ensuing stages. Concerning these events of the latter part of the action Admiral Scheer supplies much needed data, throwing new light upon manœuvres which had not been understood by the British — and no narrative has yet been published which covers this ground.

To understand the battle, it is necessary to remember that it had become the custom of the British fleet to leave its safeguarded bases in the north of the British Isles and make periodical sweeps through the North Sea. The Admiralty had ordered the Grand Fleet to begin such a sweep on May 30.[1] At the beginning of his Report of the battle Admiral Jellicoe thus describes the situation:

"The Ships of the Grand Fleet, in pursuance of the general policy of periodical sweeps through the North Sea, had left its base on the previous day in

---

[1] "In accordance with instructions contained in their Lordship's telegram, No. 434, of 30th May, code time 1740, the Grand Fleet proceeded to sea on 30th May, 1916." (J)

THE BATTLE OF JUTLAND 3

accordance with instructions issued by me. In the early afternoon of Wednesday, May 31, the 1st and 2nd Battle Cruiser Squadrons, the 1st, 2nd, and 3rd Light Cruiser Squadrons, and destroyers from the 1st, 9th, and 13th Flotillas, supported by the Fifth Battle Squadron, were, in accordance with my directions, scouting to the southward of the Battle Fleet." (J).

On May 31 the German High Seas Fleet was also on the North Sea. There had been an insistent demand from the German people for activity on the part of the battle fleet. In response, the new Commander-in-Chief, Admiral Scheer, had taken his battleships to sea at times. This change of tactics was a demonstration deliberately planned for effect in Germany, but Admiral Scheer had taken great pains to improve the efficiency of his command, and on that day he had with him all the strength he could muster, even including the available predreadnoughts. He was thus prepared to fight, if he could manœuvre to engage the British fleet in part or under conditions advantageous for the Germans. This sortie of May 31 brought on the Battle of Jutland.

For some time after the action there were tales of other objectives, — to cover the escape of raiders, to get ships out of the Baltic, etc. Even Lord

4 THE BATTLE OF JUTLAND

Jellicoe indulged in theories as to the object of the German sortie and the movements that led to the engagement. This question has been ended by Admiral Scheer's account of his definite order of May 18, 1916, for a raid on the east coast of England at Sunderland, including the dispositions of U-boats. Such a raid "would be certain to call out a display of English fighting forces as promised by Mr. Balfour." (S) After a delay on account of bad weather, this plan was modified in the operation of May 31, off the Skagerrak — and it was carried out with the hope, frankly expressed by the German Admiral, that his enemy "would afford us an opportunity to engage part or the whole of his fleet in battle under conditions favorable to ourselves." (S) This situation tended to bring on a naval action, especially as the Admiralty telegram gave the intimation that German naval forces would be out.

The opposing fleets in the Battle of Jutland were as follows:

1. An advance British force under Vice Admiral Beatty, consisting of six battle cruisers (four *Lions* of 28 knots speed, each carrying eight 13.5-inch guns, and two *Indefatigables* of 25 knots speed, each carrying eight 12-inch guns), supported by the Fifth Battle Squadron, under Rear Admiral

THE BATTLE OF JUTLAND

Evan-Thomas (four 25-knot battleships of the *Queen Elizabeth* class, each carrying eight 15-inch guns, *Barham* (F), *Valiant, Malaya, Warspite*).

The fleet speed of this advance force was 25 knots.

2. The main body of the British Grand Fleet, under Admiral Jellicoe, flying his flag in the *Iron Duke*, consisting of a fast wing under Rear Admiral Hood (three 26-knot battle cruisers of *Invincible* class, each carrying eight 12-inch guns), a division of four armored cruisers under Rear Admiral Arbuthnot, and twenty-four dreadnoughts in three squadrons commanded by Vice Admirals Burney, Jerram, and Sturdee.

The fleet speed of this main body was 20 knots, and its formidable armament will be found in Table I.

3. Twenty-five light cruisers, and seventy-eight destroyers, "47 with the Battle Fleet, 31 with Battle Cruisers." (J)

The German strength comprised:

1. An advance force under Vice Admiral Hipper, consisting of five battle cruisers (three *Derfflingers* of 28 knots speed, each carrying eight 12-inch guns, and two *Moltkes* of 27 knots speed, each carrying ten 11-inch guns).

The fleet speed of this advance force was 27 knots.

TABLE I

THE BRITISH GRAND FLEET AT THE BATTLE OF JUTLAND
Make-up and Armament of the Battle Fleet

Div.	2 D.	3 Div.	4 Div.	5 D.	6 Div.
King George V (F) 10 13.5-inch	Orion (F) 10 13.5-inch	Iron Duke (FF) 10 13.5-inch	⁵ Benbow (F) 10 13.5-inch	⁶ Colossus (F) 12 12-inch	⁷ Marlborough (F) 10 13.5-inch
Ajax 10 13.5-inch	Monarch 10 13.5-inch	Royal Oak 8 15-inch	Bellerophon 10 12-inch	Collingwood 10 12-inch	Revenge 8 15-inch
Centurion 10 13.5-inch	Conqueror 10 13.5-inch	⁴ Superb (F) 10 12-inch	Temeraire 10 12-inch	Neptune 10 12-inch	Hercules 10 12-inch
Erin 10 13.5-inch	Thunderer 10 13.5-inch	Canada 10 14-inch	Vanguard 10 12-inch	St. Vincent 10 12-inch	Agincourt 14 12-inch

¹ Fleet Flagship — Flag of Admiral Sir John Jellicoe, Commander-in-Chief.
² Flagship of Vice Admiral Sir W. C. Jerram, Commanding 2nd Battle Squadron.
³ Flagship of Rear Admiral A. C. Leveson, Rear Admiral in 2nd Battle Squadron.
⁴ Flagship of Rear Admiral A. L. Duff, Rear Admiral in 4th Battle Squadron.
⁵ Flagship of Vice Admiral Sir Doveton Sturdee, Commanding 4th Battle Squadron.
⁶ Flagship of Rear Admiral E. F. A. Gaunt, Rear Admiral in 1st Battle Squadron and second in command of the Grand Fleet.
⁷ Flagship of Vice Admiral Sir Cecil Burney, Commanding 1st Battle Squadron.

TABLE II

THE MEN HIGH SEAS FLEET AT THE BATTLE OF JUTLAND

MAKE-UP AND ARMAMENT OF THE BATTLE FLEET

Squadron III	Squadron I	Squadron II
⁴ König (F)	² Ostfriesland (F)	³ Deutschland (F)
10 12-inch	12 12-inch	4 11-inch
Grosser Kurfürst	Thüringen	Pommern
10 12-inch	12 12-inch	4 11-inch
Markgraf	Helgoland	Schlesien
10 12-inch	12 12-inch	4 11-inch
Kronprinz	Oldenburg	Schleswig-Holstein
10 12-inch	12 12-inch	4 11-inch
⁵ Kaiser (F)	⁶ Posen (F)	⁷ Hannover (F)
10 12-inch	12 11-inch	4 11-inch
Prinz Regent Luitpold	Rheinland	Hessen
10 12-inch	12 11-inch	4 11-inch
Kaiserin	Nassau	
10 12-inch	12 11-inch	
	Westfalen	
	12 11-inch	
¹ Friedrich der Grosse (FF)		
10 12-inch		

¹ Fleet Flagship — Flag of Admiral Scheer, Commander-in-Chief.
² Flagship of Vice Admiral Schmidt commanding Squadron I. ⁵ Flagship of Rear Admiral Nordmann.
³ Flagship of Rear Admiral Mauve commanding Squadron II. ⁶ Flagship of Rear Admiral Engelhardt.
⁴ Flagship of Rear Admiral Behnke commanding Squadron III. ⁷ Flagship of Rear Admiral Lichtenfels.

2. The main body of the German High Seas Fleet, under Admiral Scheer, consisting of sixteen dreadnoughts ["*König Albert* absent" (S)] and six predreadnought battleships.

The fleet speed of this main body was **17** knots, because the German dreadnoughts had been eked out with predreadnought battleships of less speed. Its less powerful armament will be found in Table II.

3. Eleven light cruisers and about seventy-eight destroyers, divided between the advance force and the main body. (Admiral Jellicoe gives the Germans eighty-eight destroyers, but it is known that all were not in action.)

The above-described make-up of the opposing fleets must be kept in mind, when studying the course of the action. The day of the battle was cloudy, but the sun shone through the clouds most of the time. At no time was there anything approaching a sea. Visibility was reported as good in the first stages of the action, but later in the afternoon, there being little wind, mist and smoke hung heavy over the surface of the sea. These conditions must also be remembered, as the increasing mist had a great influence on the course of the action.

The following outline will bring the action to the stage at which detailed comment should begin.

THE BATTLE OF JUTLAND 9

From *A Guide to the Military History of The World War, 1914-1918.*

Chart showing the Battle of Jutland, in relation to the surroundings on the North Sea. (1) The Battle Field, May 31, 1916. (2) Position of British Fleet "at about 2.47 A.M.," (J) June 1, 1916. (This chart is diagrammatic only.)

In the sweep through the North Sea, with the main body of the British Grand Fleet some seventy miles distant, Vice Admiral Beatty's advance force was cruising to southward of Admiral Jellicoe May 31, 1916, when, at 2.20 P.M., the presence of enemy ships was reported by a light cruiser. Admiral

Beatty altered course "to the eastward and subsequently to northeastward, the enemy being sighted at 3.31 P.M. Their force consisted of five battle cruisers." (B) This was the German advance under Vice Admiral Hipper.

It is stated in Vice Admiral Beatty's report that it was over an hour after the first news of the vicinity of enemy ships before he increased speed to 25 knots to engage, "at 3.30 P.M." (B) Yet Vice Admiral Beatty reports that Rear Admiral Evan-Thomas's Fifth Battle Squadron (the four *Queen Elizabeths*) was still 10,000 yards away when he made this move to engage the Germans with his battle cruisers. Consequently Vice Admiral Beatty failed to impose his whole strength upon his enemy's detached force.

It is hard to explain this situation except by believing that Vice Admiral Beatty was confident that his six battle cruisers alone would be able to cope with the enemy. Allowing his force to remain divided by such an interval was unfortunate, and it cannot be said that the best use was made of the British advance force in the first stage of the engagement.

At 3.48 "the action commenced at a range of 18,500 yards, both sides opening fire practically simultaneously." (B) The British battle cruisers fought on a course curving to the southeast, and then on a south-southeast course, and the five German battle cruisers fought them on a parallel course, instead of edging away from the superior British force. It is now easy to see that the trend of the action was absolutely in the direction of the approaching main body of the German High Seas Fleet, but this, very naturally, was not apparent at the time to Vice Admiral Beatty.

The first phase of the battle may properly be studied as a fight between the British and German battle cruisers, in consequence of the before-stated gap separating the two parts of Admiral Beatty's command. This interval of 10,000 yards prevented the Fifth Battle Squadron of *Queen Elizabeth* dreadnoughts from being a factor at the time. Vice Admiral Beatty reports that this squadron "opened fire at a range of 20,000 yards," and he continues: "The Fifth Battle Squadron was engaging the enemy's rear ships, unfortunately at very long range." Only two of the German ships were really under fire from the Fifth Battle Squadron, and these two battle cruisers were but slightly injured in the run to the south.

In this part of the action came the first of the many upsets of prewar calculations. Comparing the given strength of the two opposing squadrons in action, it will be seen that the British battle cruisers were greatly superior; in fact, the odds would have been considered prohibitive before this battle. Yet it was the British squadron that suffered, losing one-third of its ships. "At about 4.06" (J) the *Indefatigable* was sunk, and "at about 4.26" (J) the *Queen Mary* met the same fate. In each case there was a great explosion up through the turrets, suggesting that a weak turret construction is really a dangerous conductor of fire to the magazine in case of a heavy hit, and pointing to the need of better separation of the supply of ammunition from the magazine.

At 4.15 there were attacks "simultaneously" (B) by British and German destroyers which resulted in a lively fight, but no damage to any of the capital ships. Yet the possibilities of such torpedo attacks were so evident, here and later in the battle, that the destroyer at once attained a greater value as an auxiliary of the battleship. A British airplane had been sent up from a mother ship just before the engagement, though Admiral Beatty reports that it was forced to fly low on account of the clouds, and had a hard task "to identify four enemy light cruisers." (B) There was apparently no chance of a wide observation that would have warned Admiral Beatty of the approaching German High Seas Fleet. In this short hour were concentrated many new problems of naval warfare.

The advancing German High Seas Fleet was reported at 4.38 by a light cruiser, the *Southampton*, and sighted at 4.42 by the British battle cruisers. A few minutes later Vice Admiral Beatty's ships turned right about (180 degrees) in succession. The German battle cruisers also turned to a northwesterly course.

One great advantage was gained for the British in this manœuvre. By the turn in succession the four *Queen Elizabeth* battleships, the Fifth Battle Squadron, were brought into position to fight a rearguard action against the greatly strengthened force of the enemy. The leading German battleships, which were of the *König* class, fell into line, closely following Admiral Hipper's battle cruisers, and the battle was continued at 14,000 yards on a northwest course.

In the meantime, from the north, the British Grand Fleet had been closing at utmost fleet speed on south and southeast by south courses, disposed in six divisions, numbered from port to starboard, on parallel courses as shown in Table I. Admiral Jellicoe had received no certain information from Vice Admiral Beatty as to the positions of the engaged ships, and he had been proceeding in the general direction of the running fight, instead of having in mind any definite point for joining forces with Vice Admiral Beatty. It must also be realized that conditions of increasing mist and intermittent fog, which rendered observation very uncertain, had become prevalent.

It is from this stage of the action that the tactics of the battle have become involved in controversy — and a new account of the ensuing events of the battle is greatly needed.

In the first place, it should be stated that a broad tactical situation existed that was almost beyond the hopes of the British. This was irrespective of any moves of the British Commander-in-Chief, or of the Commander of the British advance force. By its own act the weaker German fleet was out in the North Sea, committed to an enterprise which had taken it away from its bases. Not only that — but, by bringing out the squadron of predreadnoughts, Admiral Scheer's fleet speed was reduced to 17 knots. Casting aside all details of tactics, this constituted the established condition that the weaker fleet of inferior speed had offered the opportunity to the British fleet — and evasion by flight alone was impossible. Looked at in this light, it was a better chance than could ever have

THE BATTLE OF JUTLAND 15

been expected. Yet a combination of circumstances, including weather conditions, tactics, and methods, prevented a decision, where such a result seemed to be insured.

This is the underlying tragedy of Jutland — and this is why all the accounts have to deal with explanations and justifications.

One very unfavorable situation was being developed at this stage, at the time when the British advance force was seeking a junction with the Grand Fleet. As has been said, Lord Jellicoe was not receiving information that would enable him to join forces effectively with Vice Admiral Beatty. The original disposition of the British naval strength, with the advance force flung ahead of the Grand Fleet, was sound, if there were tactical coördination between the separated parts. It is impossible to say that this existed, and the imperfect information given by Vice Admiral Beatty to the Commander-in-Chief is a notable feature of the battle.

With all due allowance for interference and damage to the wireless, especially on the *Lion*, it is hard to see why Lord Jellicoe should have been so badly informed as to the positions of the ships engaged, and why definite information should have been so long delayed. In this important phase of the tactics of the battle we are forced to the conclusion that all means had not been taken to insure the coördination of the British advance force and the Grand Fleet through linking up ships and other methods.

This disposition of the British forces had often been used, and the logical aim of the sweep of the North Sea was to find and engage the enemy. Yet, when the enemy actually was found, it became evident that methods had not been developed for using the whole British force as parts of one great manœuvre. With the uncertain information that Admiral Jellicoe possessed as to what was going on, any such joint manœuvre could only have taken place through a miracle of luck. As a matter of fact, there was an error of twelve miles to the eastward in location.

After the turn to the north, in the running fight in pursuit of Vice Admiral Beatty's force, the German fleet was approaching the British Grand Fleet, which drew near in the increasing mist. To understand the course of the action at this critical stage, the reader should realize that the Germans possessed a fleet manœuvre which had been carefully rehearsed for such a contingency, in sudden contact with a superior enemy force. This was a simultaneous "swing-around" (S) of all the ships of the fleet, to turn the line and bring it into an opposite course. Admiral Scheer emphasizes the pains that had been taken to develop the ability to carry out this manœuvre, which had before been considered impracticable for a fleet in action. "At our peace manœuvres great importance was always attached to their being carried out on a curved line and every means employed to ensure the working of the signals." (S) He is certainly justified in adding the statement that "the trouble spent was now well repaid," as the German Admiral was by this means enabled to carry out an unexpected and very effective manœuvre on two occasions when his fleet would have been in cramped positions without this recourse. Admiral Scheer was also able to use this identical manœuvre in an attack.

The British did not have any idea that the German Command would be able to carry out this change of direction of the German line. Consequently, in the smoke and mist, these thrice-executed movements were not suspected by the British. With such an important part of the German tactics unnoticed, and not taken into account in relation to the British movements, the reasons are evident that make necessary a new story of these phases of the action.

At this stage of the running fight, the British battle cruisers, on a northwesterly course, had drawn ahead. The four *Queen Elizabeth* battleships of Evan-Thomas's Fifth Battle Squadron were following them and "thereby played the part of cover for the badly damaged cruisers." (S) The fight had "developed into a stern chase," (S) with Hipper's battle cruisers engaging the British battle cruisers, and the German Main Fleet pressing on in chase of the Fifth Battle Squadron. The German fleet was disposed in this order: Squadron III, Squadron I, Squadron II, (pre-dreadnoughts).[1]

Squadrons III and I had opened fire at 4.45, but although they showed "speed much in excess of that for which they were designed," (J) the German battleships were gradually falling behind the fast British ships. Admiral Beatty's cruisers had drawn clear and shortly after 5.00 were free from the fire of Hipper's battle cruisers. His increase to full speed enabled Vice Admiral Beatty to draw ahead. He again opened up a gap between his battle cruisers and the Fifth Battle Squadron, taking a course that curved to the north and northeast, in search of Admiral Jellicoe's battle fleet, which was hastening to his assistance.

[1] See Table II.

The ships of the Fifth Battle Squadron were also drawing away from the German battleships and were soon only under fire from the German battle cruisers and the leading division of Squadron III. As the British battleships continued to distance their pursuers, and the fire even of this leading German division grew ineffective, Admiral Scheer at 5.20 signaled to Vice Admiral Hipper "to give chase" Hipper had already been outdistanced by the British battle cruisers. He was "forced, in order not to lose touch, to follow on the inner circle and adopt the enemy's course." (S) As Beatty swung by the north to a northeasterly direction, Hipper conformed to his course. At this stage the weather grew hazy. The wind changed from northwest to southwest, and smoke hung over the water.

The German advance was soon in a position where it could not engage to any advantage in the mist "with the sun so low on the horizon." (S) Hipper was also in danger from torpedo attacks, and at 5.40 the German Vice Admiral was compelled to turn his battle cruisers to starboard, "and finally bring the unit round to S. W." (S), to close up with the German battleships. This manœuvre was observed in the mist by the British, but not until some time after it was being carried out, as

Lord Jellicoe placed it "between 6 and 6.16." (J) At the same time the leading German battle-ships had also begun to veer around to starboard, to conform with the course of the British advance, which was swinging from northeast to an easterly direction. Observing this, Admiral Scheer states that at 5.45 the order "Leaders in Front" was signaled, "and the speed temporarily reduced to fifteen knots to make it possible for the divisions ahead, which had pushed on at high pressure, to get into position again." (S) By this means, and through the early closing up of Hipper's battle cruisers, as described, Admiral Scheer's whole command was more in hand than had been believed. The intervals were closed and the German fleet in better readiness for its rehearsed manœuvre, to change direction of the line. These alterations of speed and direction also probably increased the difficulties of the British in locating the German fleet at this time, of which Lord Jellicoe writes in describing this stage of the action.

Still thinking that the German fleet would be encountered more to the eastward, Lord Jellicoe had altered the course of the Grand Fleet to south and then to southeast. (6.02 and 6.08.) The *Lion* had been sighted, and at 6.06 had signaled that "the enemy's battle cruisers bore southeast." (J)

THE BATTLE OF JUTLAND 21

At 6.14 the *Lion* signaled, "Have sighted the enemy's battle fleet bearing south-southwest." (J) Lord Jellicoe writes· "This report gave me the first information on which I could take effective action for deployment." At 6.16 Lord Jellicoe made signal to the Grand Fleet to form line of battle on the port wing column on a course southeast by east.

In the meantime the light German forces had become involved in a fight between the lines and were withdrawing under cover of smoke screens and torpedo attacks. The cruiser *Wiesbaden* was reported disabled at 6.02, and Scheer turned his fleet two points to port "to render assistance to the *Wiesbaden*" (S) — a strange reason for such a move at such a time! This brought on what Admiral Scheer called "heavy fighting round the damaged *Wiesbaden*," from 6.20. Yet this eccentric thrust of the German fleet actually resulted in heavy damage to the British.

At this time the Grand Fleet was deploying as described, but not yet seriously engaged. Lord Jellicoe reports the *Marlborough* as opening fire at 6.17, the *Iron Duke* firing a few salvos at 6.20. But Vice Admiral Beatty's four remaining battle cruisers were in closer action, as Beatty was crossing the German van on a course turning from east to southeast. The speed of the deploying Grand

Fleet had been reduced to 14 knots to allow Beatty's cruisers to pass ahead, "as there was danger of the fire of the Battle Fleet being blanketed by them." (J) The Fifth Battle Squadron had been left behind Beatty's battle cruisers by a long interval, and was making a turn to port (at 6.19) to form astern of the Grand Fleet.

Rear Admiral Hood's Third Squadron of three battle cruisers which had been ordered to reinforce Beatty's advance, was far ahead of the Grand Fleet, and had overrun to the southeast in the error as to location. On realizing this mistake, Hood had turned back in the direction of the British advance. Hood's squadron was signaled by Vice Admiral Beatty "to form single line ahead and take station" (J) ahead of Admiral Beatty's four remaining battle cruisers, which were turned to a southeast and southerly course across the van of the German fleet. In obedience to this signal, Rear Admiral Hood turned to take station ahead (6.21), closing to a range of 8,000 yards (6.25). "At about 6.34" (J) his flagship, the *Invincible*, was sunk by gunfire.

Almost at the same time three of Rear Admiral Arbuthnot's armored cruisers, *Black Prince*, *Warrior*, and *Defence*, "not aware of the approach of the enemy's heavy ships," (J) were put out of action. (*Defence* was sunk; *Warrior* sank while attempt was being made to tow her home; *Black Prince* was sunk later.) In the turn of the Fifth Battle Squadron to take position astern of the Grand Fleet the *Warspite* had jammed her helm and was out of control for a while. She was a good deal damaged by gunfire, but was extricated from her predicament and taken back to the British base.

By this time the German Commander-in-Chief had received information from his torpedo flotillas of the presence of "more than twenty enemy battleships following a southerly course." (S) His van was under heavy fire. "Following the movements of the enemy they had made a bend which hindered free action" (S) of his torpedo flotilla, and his cruisers were also cramped between the fire of both lines. In this awkward situation Admiral Scheer resolved to make use of his prepared manœuvre, to change the direction of his line. Accordingly at 6.35 "the swing-around was carried out in excellent style," (S) the ships turning simultaneously to starboard, putting the whole German fleet on a westerly course.

This manœuvre was covered by the use of dense smoke screens, and the pressure on the German fleet was relieved at once. Admiral Scheer states that "the enemy did not follow our veer around," and he strongly insists that the British should have held firmly to his line by executing a similar manœuvre. But he really gives the true state of the case when he writes: "It may be that the leader did not grasp the situation." In fact none of the British commanders realized what had taken place under cover of that smoke screen.

After the sinking of the *Invincible*, although Vice Admiral Beatty was reported as turning to starboard, there was no further aggressive action on his part — and, in the next fifteen minutes (6.50), he signaled the two remaining battle cruisers of the Third Squadron to take station astern of the last ship of his line, the *New Zealand.*

At the same time (6.50) the Grand Fleet, which had completed deployment at 6.38, altered course to south by divisions to close.

These movements of the British forces naturally did not succeed in bringing any pressure upon the Germans, as Admiral Scheer's whole fleet was then safely on a westerly course, as a result of the simultaneous swing-around of his line — and the German fleet was concealed by dense smoke screens, which left the British in ignorance of Scheer's manœuvre. Encouraged by this successful result of his move, and finding his ships all able to keep their places in the line, "fully prepared to fight," (S) the German Admiral decided upon an unexpected course of action. His change of tactics was so remarkable that his reasons should be quoted at length:

"It was still too early for a nocturnal move. If the enemy followed us, our action in retaining the direction taken after turning the line would partake of the nature of a retreat, and in the event of any damage to our ships in the rear the Fleet would be compelled to sacrifice them or else to decide on a line of action enforced by enemy pressure, and not adopted voluntarily, and would therefore be detrimental to us from the very outset. Still less was it feasible to strive at detaching oneself from the enemy, leaving him to decide when he could elect to meet us the next morning. There was but one way of averting this — to force the enemy into a second battle by another determined advance, and forcibly compel his torpedo boats to attack. The success of the turning of the line while fighting encouraged me to make the attempt, and decided me to make still further use of the facility of movement. The manœuvre would be bound to surprise the enemy, to upset his plans for the rest of the day, and if the blow fell heavily it would facilitate the breaking loose at night." (S)

To carry out these ideas Admiral Scheer at 6.55 executed a second swing-around of his whole fleet turning ships-right-about to starboard as before. This put the German fleet again on an easterly course and launched its van in an attack against the deployed British line, "to deal a blow at the centre of the enemy's line." (S) Ahead of the fleet there was sent forward a determined attack by the German torpedo flotillas, all of which "had orders to attack." (S) In the words of Admiral Scheer, "This led to the intended result, a full resumption of the firing at the van."

The practical effect in action, so far as the German Battle Fleet was concerned, was to subject the van of the German fleet to heavy damage, without doing any compensating harm to the British ships. Admiral Scheer admits this damage to the German fleet, especially the battle cruisers, and it is established that the German fleet did not score upon the Grand Fleet. On the other hand, the accompanying sudden torpedo attacks, emerging from the smoke directed against the British battleships, did actually accomplish the result of making the Grand Fleet turn away and open the range. Admiral Scheer claims that putting the van of his fleet again into action "diverted the enemy fire and rendered it possible for the torpedoboat flotillas to take so effective a share in the proceedings," (S) but of course it is a question whether the same result might not have been obtained by the use of the torpedo flotillas alone.

In any case, it must be acknowledged that Admiral Scheer's extraordinary manœuvres had accomplished a surprise effect upon his enemy as, besides forcing the Grand Fleet to turn away, the moral effect of this torpedo attack had a great influence upon the British conduct of the rest of the action. It is also evident that the British had not comprehended the tactics of the Germans.

One phase of the situation at this time has not been understood — but should be strongly emphasized. The fact is that the German Admiral, by his own act, had again placed his fleet in the same position from which he had once withdrawn — and this second creation of the same situation (6.55) was *after* the Grand Fleet had deployed and was in line of battle. Consequently, in view of the way the battle was really fought, many of the long arguments as to the so-called crucial situation at the time of the British deployment are wasted words. Now that it is known that Admiral Scheer came back again to attack the fully deployed British fleet, the much-discussed method of deployment can no longer be considered all-important. Even if the deployment had not come to the Germans, the Germans had gone to the deployment — and the same situation existed. In their ignorance of the German Admiral's smoke-screened manœuvres, both sides of the heated British controversy have missed the essential fact of this unusual duplication of a battle situation, which actually occurred at Jutland.

This lack of understanding of Scheer's turn and return is plainly shown by Admiral Jellicoe, who writes, concerning the situation after 7.00: "Our alteration of course to the south had, meanwhile, brought the enemy's line into view once more." The British Command did not realize that his enemy had actually voluntarily come back into the former position, and this was the real reason the German ships had reappeared.

At 7.05 the whole British battle line had been turned together three more points to starboard. But at 7.10 the sudden attack of the German torpedo flotillas was sighted, and shortly afterwards the British fleet was turned away to port two points, and then two points more, to avoid the run of the torpedoes. Admiral Jellicoe states that this move enabled his battleships to avoid many torpedoes, and that the range was opened by about 1,750 yards. The German Admiral claims

After accomplishing this result of making his enemy turn away, Admiral Scheer at 7.17 for a third time successfully executed the same manœuvre of ships-right-about (in this third turn Scheer's flagship, *Friedrich der Grosse*, was cramped and made the turn to port), and again his fleet was on a westerly course screened by dense smoke. This swing-around again had the same effect of freeing the German fleet from the gunfire of the British fleet. The British Command again did not grasp the full import of the German move. He writes of the difficulty of observation in the mist and smoke. Some of his subordinates reported that the Germans had turned away at this time, but none realized that a ships-right-about had been carried out. It was not until 7.41 that the British battle fleet was altered by divisions three points to starboard to close.

Shortly after (at 7.47), Vice Admiral Beatty made signal to Lord Jellicoe: "Urgent. Submit that the van of battleships follow the cruisers. We can then cut off the whole of the enemy's battle fleet." Much has been made of this signal by ill-advised critics. In fact it will be self-evident that, at the time Beatty's signal was sent, the German fleet was not in the assumed position, but had long before been extricated from its dangerous contact by the third "swing-around" (S) at 7.17, and the Germans ships were again safely proceeding on their altered course.

It is a strange comment on the battle to realize that the thrice executed German manœuvre of ships-right-about was not observed by anyone on the British fleet. None of the British maps or charts of the action shows any sign of these movements. Chart No. 1 is a typical British diagram of this stage of the action. It will be noted that the times (6.15 to 7.41) in the indications of the course of the German fleet include the times of all three turns of ships-right-about. (6.35, 6.55, 7.17.) Yet there is no trace of these German manœuvres on the plan. Chart No. 2 shows the contrast between the supposed movements of the Germans and their actual manœuvres in the battle.

One reason for the failure of the British to understand these manœuvres of Admiral Scheer was the fixed conviction of the British that such a simultaneous turn of all the ships of a fleet was impracticable in action — consequently they did not expect it to be used by their enemies. This doctrine has been stated by Lord Jellicoe in explaining

THE BATTLE OF JUTLAND

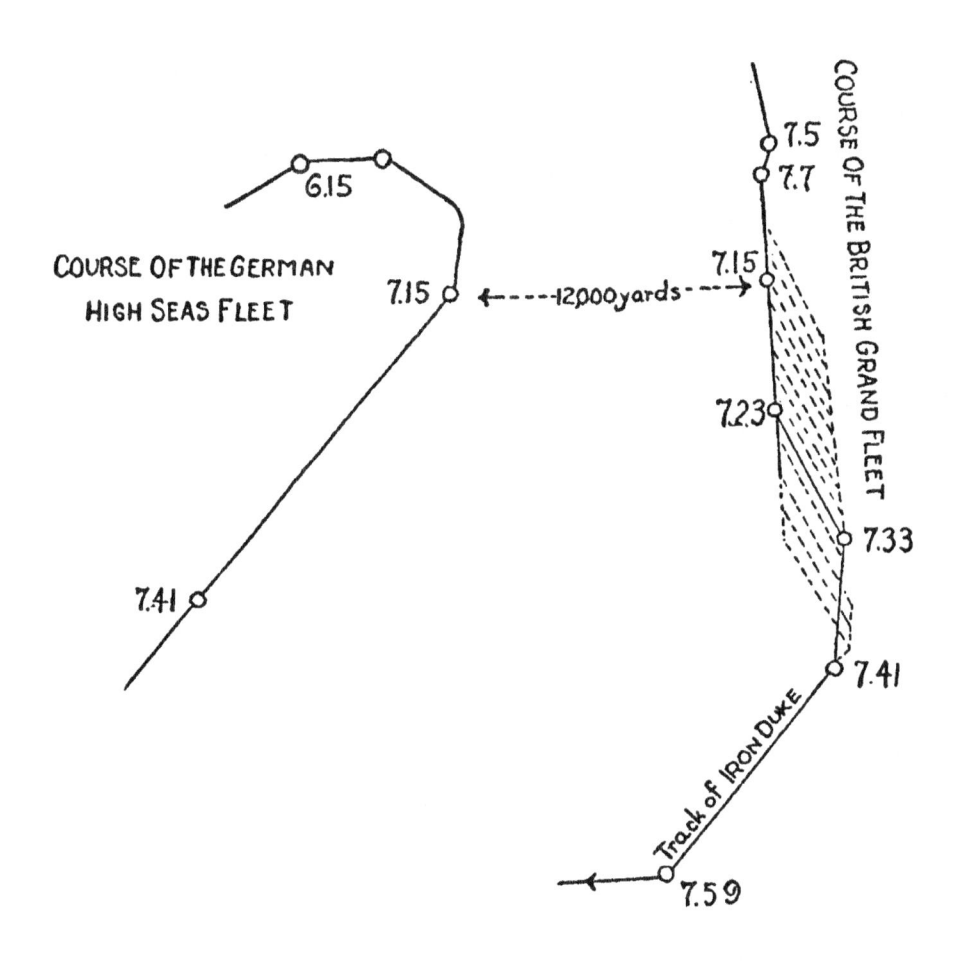

CHART NO. 1

Typical British Chart, of the later manœuvres of the action which are in dispute.

It will be noted that, in the time covered, between 6.15 and 7.41, the course of the German Fleet gives no indication of the thrice executed change of direction of the German line by ships-right-about. All of these were carried out within this period (6.35, 6.55, 7.17).

Lord Jellicoe's own maps show this lack of knowledge of the German manœuvres of ships-right-about, as they do not indicate these important moves of the Germans. In his report Admiral Jellicoe spoke of the "turn-away under cover of torpedo-boat destroyer attacks" (J) as "difficult to counter" (J)—but he did not understand the real reason that made the difficulty.

his own movements in the battle. "The objection to altering by turning all the ships together was the inevitable confusion that would have ensued as the result of such a manœuvre carried out with a very large fleet under action conditions in misty weather." This positive statement was made by the British Commander-in-Chief in perfect unconsciousness that his antagonist had in fact successfully carried out such a turn three times under the identical conditions described!

After the turn to a westerly course, the German fleet was brought around to a southwesterly, southerly, and finally to a southeasterly course "to meet the enemy's encircling movements and keep open a way for our return." (S) From this time Admiral Scheer's fleet was not in great danger, nor even seriously engaged. As the twilight advanced the German Command could prepare for the night. He found all his battleships in condition to do 16 knots "the speed requisite for night work, and thus keep their places in the line." (S) Vice Admiral Hipper's flagship the *Lützow* had been so badly damaged that he had changed his flag to the *Moltke* (7.00).[1] At 7.30 the *Lützow* could do 15 knots, and her condition grew worse steadily, but

[1] It was nearly two hours before Vice Admiral Hipper could get on board the *Moltke*.

she was the only ship that could not be relied upon to maintain fleet speed.

Consequently Admiral Scheer was not hard pressed at this stage, but only intermittently engaged. The order of the German fleet, after the last turn to westerly, had been Squadron II, Squadron I, Squadron III. Squadron II (the slower predreadnoughts) fell out to starboard, and was passed by Squadrons I and III, giving support to Hipper's battle cruisers, which were engaged at 8.20. The Germans were all the time making use of smoke for concealment, in addition to the mist and the increasing darkness.

As a result of these tactics, the British Admiral was always groping for his enemy in mist and smoke, with only occasional glimpses of the German ships. Although he had not understood the German manœuvre, Lord Jellicoe had become convinced that the Germans had turned away, and at 7.59 he had altered course by divisions to west to close his enemy. It was again natural that he did not gain much actual contact. Lord Jellicoe writes of the fighting, already mentioned, at 8.20, in which the battle cruisers of both sides and the German predreadnoughts were engaged, and explains the puzzling conditions of the action at this stage. "At 8.30 P.M. the light was failing and the fleet was turned by divisions to a southwest course, thus reforming single line again." (J) All this time his elusive enemy was screening his movements by the use of smoke, and the German ships would only occasionally be visible in the smoke and mist.

As the darkness came on, it is evident that these tactics on the part of the Germans, with increasing threats of torpedo attacks, became more and more baffling to the British Command, and then came the crucial decision which ended the battle. Admiral Jellicoe reports:

"At 9 P.M. the enemy was entirely out of sight, and the threat of torpedoboat-destroyer attacks during the rapidly approaching darkness made it necessary for me to dispose of the fleet for the night, with a view to its safety from such attacks, while providing for a renewal of action at daylight. I accordingly manœuvred to remain between the enemy and his bases, placing our flotillas in a position in which they would afford protection to the fleet from destroyer attack and at the same time be favorably situated for attacking the enemy's heavy ships."

Concerning this stage of the action Admiral Jellicoe in his report quotes Vice Admiral Beatty as follows: "In view of the gathering darkness and the fact that our strategical position was such as to make it appear certain that we should locate the enemy at daylight under most favorable circumstances, I did not consider it desirable or proper to close the enemy battle-fleet during the dark hours."

Here the British Admiral and his subordinate were in accord, but of course the responsibility for the movements of the British fleet rested with Admiral Jellicoe, as Commander-in-Chief. By his order the British fleet steamed through the dark hours on southerly courses "some eighty-five miles" (J) from the battlefield. Although the British fleet was thus placed in the general direction of Heligoland, this meant that Admiral Jellicoe relinquished contact, in a military sense, with the German fleet. At the time it was undoubtedly Lord Jellicoe's intention to renew the action the next day, but it must be clearly understood that this was to be in every way a new naval battle — not a battle continued by keeping in touch with his enemy and reëxerting his force on the following day.

Admiral Jellicoe himself is explicit upon this point, and states that "at 9 P.M." he ordered his fleet "to alter course by divisions to *south*, informing the Flag officers of the Battle Cruiser Fleet, the cruiser and light cruiser squadrons, and the officers commanding destroyer flotillas, of my movements in order that they should conform." (J) Nothing could be more definitely established than the fact that this broke off the action of fleets in every real sense of the word. The British light craft were to conform to the movements of the Battle Fleet, and there was no hint of maintaining a screen or contact that would develop the position of the enemy fleet.

This situation should be kept clearly in mind. There were many encounters throughout the night between British and German war-craft of various types, but these fought on their own initiative, and there was no concerted touch maintained with the German fleet — nothing that could be called a part of a battle of fleets. The Germans simply ploughed their way home through the stragglers left in the wake of the British fleet, and Lord Jellicoe frankly states that he was out of touch with his cruisers and destroyers. Consequently Lord Jellicoe's decision, and move to the south, ended the Battle of Jutland.

This should be recognized as the final decision of the battle, and the British Commander-in-Chief makes it plain that he so considered it, as he states the situation at the time and the reasons which influenced him.

At 9 o'clock the German fleet was to the westward. The British fleet was between it and all its bases. The British fleet was superior in speed, and had such an overwhelming superiority in ships and guns that it could afford to discard its damaged ships without impairing this superiority. The British Admiral had light cruisers and destroyers, to throw out a screen and to maintain touch with the German fleet. There was a proportion of damaged ships in the German fleet; and this, with its original inferior fleet speed, would have made it a hard task for the German fleet to ease around the British fleet and reach the German bases. These conditions were in favor of keeping in touch with the German fleet.

On the other hand, for Admiral Jellicoe to have kept his fleet in touch with the German fleet through the dark hours, even by the most efficient use of his screen of destroyers and cruisers, would have meant taking the risk of a night action, which would have involved his capital ships, as Admiral Scheer intended to fight his way through that night. Above all things there was the ominous threat of torpedo attacks in the night, with possibilities of disaster to the Battle Fleet upon which depended the established British control of the seas.

Lord Jellicoe's arguments show that he followed a line of conduct well considered in advance,[1] and he writes with a sincere conviction that his act in breaking off the battle was justified by the results. In explaining the many advantages possessed by the weaker German fleet Admiral Jellicoe also reveals disappointing conditions in backwardness of methods on the part of the British Navy. There was not alone the lack of modern methods in range-finding and director fire-control, but also in torpedo attack and defense, and in preparation for action "under night conditions." (J)[2] It is something of a shock to read that the stronger British fleet went into the Jutland battle with a handicap in these essentials that became a factor to prevent a decisive action.[3] Lord Jellicoe makes a very strong

---

[1] Lord Jellicoe had sent to the Admiralty a formal dispatch (October 30, 1914) stating his conviction that the Germans would "rely to a great extent on submarines, mines and torpedoes," (J) and defining his own "tactical methods in relation to these forms of attack." (J) On November 7, 1914, the Admiralty approved the "views stated therein." Lord Jellicoe in his book cites this Admiralty approval of 1914 as applying to the Battle of Jutland.

[2] "The German organization at night is very good. Their system of recognition signals is excellent. Ours are practically nil. Their searchlights are superior to ours, and they use them with great effect. Finally, their method of firing at night gives excellent results. I am reluctantly of the opinion that under night conditions we have a good deal to learn from them." (J)

[3] "The British Fleet was not properly equipped for fighting an action at night. The German fleet was. Consequently to fight

THE BATTLE OF JUTLAND 39

plea for his contention that, under the existing conditions of smoke, mist and darkness, with the German fleet skilfully taking advantage of these conditions, and with the handicaps of the Grand Fleet in construction, equipment, and methods to contend with these tactics and conditions, there was no opportunity to force a decision without prohibitive risks of losing the existing supremacy of the British Navy on the seas.[1]

Accordingly, at 9 o'clock Admiral Jellicoe disposed the British battleships for the night in columns of divisions abeam one mile apart, to insure the columns not losing sight of one another through the dark hours. The destroyer flotillas were directed to take station five miles astern. In this order the British fleet steamed through the night at seventeen knots "some 85 miles" (J) on a southerly course. The only British ship that is mentioned as having been given another mission was the small minelayer *Abdiel* which was sent to strew mines in an area off the Vyl Lightship "over which it was expected the High Seas Fleet would pass if the ships attempted to regain their

them at night would only have been to court disaster. Lord Jellicoe's business was to preserve the Grand Fleet, the main defense of the Empire as well as of the Allied cause, not to risk its existence." Sir Percy Scott, *Fifty Years in the Royal Navy*.

[1] See *A Guide to the Military History of The World War*, pp. 320-22.

ports during the night via the Horn Reef." (J) No other craft was assigned to observe or harass the German fleet. The Sixth Division of the Grand Fleet had fallen behind, as the *Marlborough*, which had been damaged by a torpedo, could not maintain fleet speed. (This ship had to be sent back after 2 A.M., and Sir Cecil Burney transferred his flag to the *Revenge*.) The British light craft also became widely scattered in the dark hours.

Within a few minutes of the time of Lord Jellicoe's signal for the move to the south, Admiral Scheer gave his order for the night (9.06), "course S. S. E. ¼ E. speed 16 knots." (S) The German Admiral fully expected to be attacked by the British fleet and to meet strong opposition, but he decided that the German "main fleet in close formation was to make for Horn Reef by the shortest route." (S) The fleet was disposed in the same order, Squadrons I, III, II, with the battle cruisers covering the rear — "out of consideration for their damaged condition." (S) The German Admiral placed these weaker ships in the rear, as he thought his van would encounter resistance and might be heavily engaged in the expected night action. His torpedo flotillas were disposed "in an E. N. E. to S. S. W. direction, which was where the enemy Main Fleet could be expected." (S)

Thus disposed the German Battle Fleet moved through the dark hours, on a straight course for Horn Reef, without meeting the expected attacks, which the strong Squadron I in the van was prepared to ward off. There really was no chance of engaging the British battleships, as the Grand Fleet had moved to the south before the German fleet crossed Lord Jellicoe's course. The *Nassau* got out of station, when she struck a stray British destroyer in the darkness, and made for a morning rendezvous. The rest of the dreadnoughts of the High Seas Fleet met no delay nor mishap through the dark hours. Of the predreadnoughts, the battleship *Pommern* was sunk by a mine or torpedo, with loss of all hands.

Many of the destroyers had fired all their torpedoes, and these craft were used for emergencies. They were very necessary, as the disabled cruisers *Rostock* and *Elbing* were abandoned and blown up, and these destroyers did good service in taking off the crews. They also rescued the crew of the disabled *Lützow*, which was towed through the darkness until she was so down by the head that her screws spun in the air. She was abandoned and destroyed by a torpedo at 1.45 A.M. Admiral Scheer cites the fact that these events could happen, without disturbance by the enemy, as "proving that the English Naval forces made no attempt to occupy the waters between the scene of battle and Horn Reef." (S)

As a matter of fact this did not need any proof, because the British fleet held steadily on its southerly course, without regard to the direction taken by the Germans. In the wake of the Grand Fleet were left scattered cruisers and destroyers — and there were many clashes between these and the Germans, but all were isolated fights and adventures of lame ducks. Some of these encounters were reported to Lord Jellicoe and there was much shooting, with explosions and fire lighting up the darkness.

Admiral Scheer thought that all this must have indicated his position, and, even after not encountering the expected night attacks, the German Admiral expected the British to renew the battle promptly at dawn. But in consequence of the British Admiral's dispositions for the night, it is evident that the position of the German fleet was not developed, as Admiral Jellicoe himself says, until "the information obtained from our wireless directional stations during the early morning." (J)

As dawn was breaking, "at about 2.47 A.M." (J) June 1, Admiral Jellicoe altered course of his fleet to the north to retrace his path of the night before.

His Sixth Division of battleships had dropped astern, out of sight. His cruisers and destroyers were badly scattered, and the British Admiral abandoned his intention of seeking a new battle on the first of June.

The straggling of portions of his fleet during the move through the darkness is explained by Lord Jellicoe, and this caused him to delay his search for the German fleet until he could pick up the missing craft. His return to find these was the reason for retracing the course of the night manœuvre. The following is quoted from Lord Jellicoe's book: "The difficulty experienced in collecting the fleet (particularly the destroyers), due to the above causes, rendered it undesirable for the Battle Fleet to close the Horn Reef at daylight, as had been my intention when deciding to steer to the southward during the night. It was obviously necessary to concentrate the Battle Fleet and the destroyers before renewing action. By the time this concentration was effected it had become apparent that the High Seas Fleet, steering for the Horn Reef, had passed behind the shelter of the German mine fields in the early morning on their way to their ports."

Admiral Scheer's fleet had arrived off Horn Reef at 3 A.M., where he waited for the disabled *Lützow*.

At 3.30 he learned that she had been abandoned. Up to that time the German Admiral had expected a new battle of fleets, but he soon divined that he was to be free from pressure on the part of his enemy. This was confirmed when Admiral Scheer learned through a German aircraft scout of the straggling of Lord Jellicoe's ships. (L 11 was the airship reported by the British "shortly after 3.30.") Admiral Scheer's comment is: "It is obvious that this scattering of the forces — which can only be explained by the fact that after the day-battle Admiral Jellicoe had lost the general command — induced the Admiral to avoid a fresh battle." Both commanders are consequently on record in agreement as to the reason for no new battle of fleets.

The Germans were thus enabled to proceed to their bases undisturbed. Admiral Scheer's account of the return of the German fleet to its home ports, and of the condition of his ships, is convineing — and there is no longer any question as to the German losses. On the way home the *Ostfriesland* struck a mine, but was not seriously injured, making port without difficulty. Outside of the destruction of the *Lützow*, the German battle cruiser squadron was badly battered. The *Seydlitz* had great difficulty in making her berth, and

THE BATTLE OF JUTLAND

the *Derfflinger* was also seriously damaged. To sum up the damage done to the battle cruisers of both fleets makes a sorry showing for this type of warship, which had so great a vogue before The World War.

Admiral Scheer states that, with the exception of his two battle cruisers, the German fleet was repaired and ready to go to sea again by the middle of August, and the *Bayern* (the first German warship to mount 38 c.m.-guns) had been added to the fleet. He also gives an account of another sortie (August 18 to 20, 1916). Later in the year the German fleet was reinforced by the *Baden* (38 c.m.-guns) and the battle cruiser *Hindenburg*, but at the end of 1916 the function of the High Seas Fleet was to keep the gates for the U-boats in the great German submarine campaign.

In this rôle of covering the operations of the submarines the German Battle Fleet had a very important influence upon the ensuing stages of the War. It was altogether a delusion to think that the career of the German fleet had been ended at Jutland — and that it "never came out." On the contrary, Admiral Scheer's fleet kept a wide area cleared for the egress and entrance of the German U-boats in their destructive campaign. If the German fleet had been destroyed in the

Jutland action, it would have been possible for the Allies to put in place and maintain mine barrages close to the German bases. There is no need to add anything to this statement to show the great results that would have been gained, if the British had been able to win a decision in the Battle of Jutland.

The losses in the battle were as follows:

BRITISH

		Tons
QUEEN MARY	(*Battle Cruiser*)	26,350
INDEFATIGABLE	(*Battle Cruiser*)	18,800
INVINCIBLE	(*Battle Cruiser*)	17,250
DEFENCE	(*Armored Cruiser*)	14,600
WARRIOR	(*Armored Cruiser*)	13,550
BLACK PRINCE	(*Armored Cruiser*)	13,350
TIPPERARY	(*Destroyer*)	1,430
NESTOR	(*Destroyer*)	890
NOMAD	(*Destroyer*)	890
TURBULENT	(*Destroyer*)	1,100
FORTUNE	(*Destroyer*)	965
ARDENT	(*Destroyer*)	935
SHARK	(*Destroyer*)	935
SPARROWHAWK	(*Destroyer*)	935
	Total tonnage	111,980

GERMAN

		Tons
LÜTZOW	(*Battle Cruiser*)	26,180
POMMERN	(*Predreadnought*)	13,200
WIESBADEN	(*Cruiser*)	5,400
ELBING	(*Cruiser*)	4,500
ROSTOCK	(*Cruiser*)	4,900
FRAUENLOB	(*Cruiser*)	2,700

		Tons
V-4	(*Destroyer*)	570
V-48	(*Destroyer*)	750
V-27	(*Destroyer*)	640
V-29	(*Destroyer*)	640
S-33	(*Destroyer*)	700
	Total tonnage	60,180

Killed and wounded:
    British (approximately)   6,600
    German   3,076

In the early British accounts of the battle there were fanciful tales of pursuit of the German ships, through the night, and even after Admiral Jellicoe's Report the British public did not at first realize the situation at the end of the action. But after a time, when this was better understood, there arose one of the greatest naval controversies that have ever agitated Great Britain, centered around the alleged "defensive" naval policy for maintaining the supremacy of Great Britain on the seas, — the pros and cons as to closing the Germans while there was light, and keeping in touch through the dark hours.

This controversy as to the Battle of Jutland has been carried on with bitterness in Great Britain, and volumes of matter have been written that will be utterly useless, so far as a true story of the action is concerned. Partisans have made the mistake of putting on record arguments that have been founded on phases of the British operations —

with imaginary corresponding situations of the enemy, which never existed in actual fact. The preceding account may be relied upon as tracing the main events of the battle — and the real course of the action shows that many briefs must be thrown out of court.

Putting aside these contentions, and seeking only to visualize the truth, one is forced to the conclusion that the chief cause of failure on the part of the British fleet was the obvious handicap that methods had not been devised in advance for decisive operations under the existing conditions.

The problem for the British was to unite two parts of a superior force, and to impose this united superior force with destructive effect upon the enemy. This problem was simplified by the fact that the weaker enemy voluntarily came into contact in a position where escape by flight was out of the question. On the other hand, the solution was made difficult by unusual conditions of mist and smoke.

The decision was missed through the lack of rehearsed methods, not only for effectively joining the British forces, but for bringing into contact the superior British strength, against an enemy who actually possessed the great advantage of rehearsed methods adapted to the existing conditions.

These conditions must be realized in order to arrive at a fair verdict.

When considering the Battle of Jutland, we must not think in the old terms of small dimensions, but we must picture the long miles of battle lines wreathed in mist and smoke, the great areas of manœuvre — and the complicated difficulties that must beset anyone who was called to command in this first great battle of dreadnoughts. These widely extended manœuvres of ships, only intermittently visible, must not be thought of as merely positions on a chart or game-board.

Reviewing the course of the action, the conclusion cannot be avoided that, on the day of the battle and under its conditions, the Germans were better prepared in advance for a battle of fleets. In his book Lord Jellicoe states many advantages possessed by the German fleet in construction, armament, and equipment — but, as has been said, his revelation of the British lack of methods is more significant.

All these deficiencies cannot be charged against Admiral Jellicoe, and the persistent efforts to give him all the blame are unjust. Is there any real evidence that another man would have done better under the circumstances? The tendency of certain writers to laud Vice Admiral Beatty at the expense of Admiral Jellicoe does not seem justified. As has been noted, when contact was established with the German advance force, Beatty failed to bring his full strength into action against this isolated weaker enemy force. In the ensuing stages it cannot be denied that haphazard methods were in evidence.

The idea must be put aside that the German ships were a huddled, helpless prey "delivered" to the British Commander-in-Chief. On the contrary, as stated, the German battle cruisers had already closed up with the German battleships and the High Seas Fleet had been slowed down to correct its formations. Consequently at this stage the German fleet was in hand and ready to sheer off, by use of their well rehearsed elusive manœuvre of ships-right-about, with baffling concealment in smoke screens. It has been shown that *after* the Grand Fleet had completed deployment, the unsuspected situation existed in which Admiral Scheer's fleet was again in close contact with the British fleet. It has also been explained that Vice Admiral Beatty made his much discussed signal, to "cut off" the German fleet, long after Admiral Scheer had put his fleet into safety by his third swing-around of the German ships. With these situations totally uncomprehended, it cannot be said that Vice Admiral Beatty had a firmer grasp upon the actual conditions than anyone else. The simple truth is, the British Command was always compelled to grope for the German ships, while his enemies were executing carefully rehearsed elusive manœuvres concealed in smoke — and the British were not prepared in advance to counter these tactics.

In the matter of signaling, the Germans were far ahead — in that they had their manœuvres carefully prepared in advance, to be executed with the minimum number of signals. The result was that, while the British Commander-in-Chief was obliged to keep up a constant succession of in structions by signals, the German Admiral was able to perform his surprising manœuvres with comparatively few master signals.[1] Lord Jellicoe also emphasizes the great advantage possessed by the Germans in their recognition signals at night.

Sir Percy Scott, as already quoted, bluntly states: "The British Fleet was not properly equipped for fighting an action at night. The German Fleet was." To this should be added the statement that the British fleet was not prepared

[1] "Jellicoe was sending out radio instructions at the rate of two a minute — while von Scheer made only *nine* such signals during the whole battle. This I learn on credible testimony." Rear Admiral Caspar F. Goodrich, U.S.N.

in methods in advance to cope with the conditions of the afternoon of May 31. The German fleet was. Herein lay the chief cause for failure to gain a decision, when the one great opportunity of the war was offered to the British fleet.

In the three decades before The World War great strides had been made in naval development, with only the unequal fighting in the American War with Spain and in the East to give the tests of warfare. In this period it is probable that at different times first one navy would be in the lead and then another. It was the misfortune of the British in the Battle of Jutland that the Germans, at that time, were better prepared in equipment and rehearsed methods for an action under the existing conditions. This should be recognized as an important factor — and the failure to win a decision should not be wholly charged against the men who fought the battle.

The destroyer came to its own in the Battle of Jutland as an auxiliary of the battle fleet, both for offense and defense. The whole course of the action proved that a screen of destroyers was absolutely necessary. For offense, it might be argued truthfully that, of the great number of torpedoes used, very few hit anything. The *Marlborough* was the only capital ship reported struck in the

THE BATTLE OF JUTLAND 53

real action,[1] and she was able afterward to take some part in the battle, and then get back to her base. But above all things stands out the fact that it was the threat of night torpedo attacks by German destroyers, and the desire to safeguard the British capital ships from these torpedo attacks, which made the British fleet withdraw from the battlefield, and break off touch with the German fleet. Lord Jellicoe states that he "rejected at once the idea of a night action" on account of "first the presence of torpedo craft in such large numbers." (J)

There is no question of the fact that this withdrawal of the British fleet had a great moral effect on Germany. Morale was all-important in The World War, and the announcement to the people and to the Reichstag had a heartening effect on the Germans at just the time they needed some such stimulant, with an unfavorable military situation for the Central Powers. It also smoothed over the irritation of the German people against the German Navy, at this time when Germany had been obliged to modify her use of the U-boats upon the demand of the United States. For months after the battle the esteem of the German

[1] The *Pommern* was sunk in the night after the action of fleets had been broken off.

people for the German Navy remained high, and this helped to strengthen the German Government. But the actual tactical result of the battle was indecisive. It may be said that the Germans had so manœuvred their fleet that a detached part of the superior British force was cut up, but the damage was not enough to impair the established superiority of the British fleet.

As a matter of fact the Battle of Jutland did not have any actual effect upon the situation on the seas. The British fleet still controlled the North Sea. The Entente Allies were still able to move their troops and supplies over water-ways which were barred to the Germans. Not a German ship was released from port, and there was no effect upon the blockade. After Jutland, as before, the German fleet could not impose its power upon the seas, and it could not make any effort to end the blockade. The Jutland action had cheered the German people but it had not given to Germany even a fragment of sea power.

CHART NO. 2
THE BATTLE OF JUTLAND
(This chart is diagrammatic only)

Most of the published narratives have used many charts to trace the events of the action. It has been found possible to indicate all the essentials upon this one chart, which has been so placed that it can be opened outside the pages for use as the text is being read. It should be noted that superimposed indications have been avoided, where ships passed over the same areas (especially in the three German ships-right-about manoeuvres). Consequently this chart is diagrammatic only.

I. BATTLE CRUISER ACTION

① 3.30 P.M. Beatty sights Hipper.

② 3.48 P.M. Battle cruisers engage at 18,500 yds., "both forces opening fire practically simultaneously."

③ 4.06 P.M. *Indefatigable* sunk.

④ 4.42 P.M. Beatty sights High Seas Fleet, and turns north (column right about).

⑤ 4.57 P.M. Evan-Thomas turns north, covering Beatty.

⑥ 5.35 P.M. Beatty's force, pursued by German battle cruisers and High Seas Fleet, on northerly course at long range.

II. MAIN ENGAGEMENT

⑦ 5.56 P.M. Beatty sights Jellicoe and shifts to easterly course at utmost speed.

⑧ 6.20-7.00 P.M. Jellicoe deploys on port wing column (deployment "complete" at 6.38). Beatty takes position ahead of Grand Fleet. Hood takes station ahead of Beatty. Evan-Thomas falls in astern of Grand Fleet.

Scheer turns whole German Fleet to west (ships right about) at 6.35, covered by smoke screens. Scheer repeats the turn of the whole fleet (ships right about) to east at 6.55.

⑨ 7.17 P.M. Scheer for the third time makes "swing-around" of whole German Fleet (ships right about) to southwest, under cover of smoke screens and destroyer attacks. Jellicoe turns away to avoid torpedoes (7.23).

⑩ 8.00 P.M.

⑪ 8.30-9.00 P.M. Jellicoe disposes for the night.

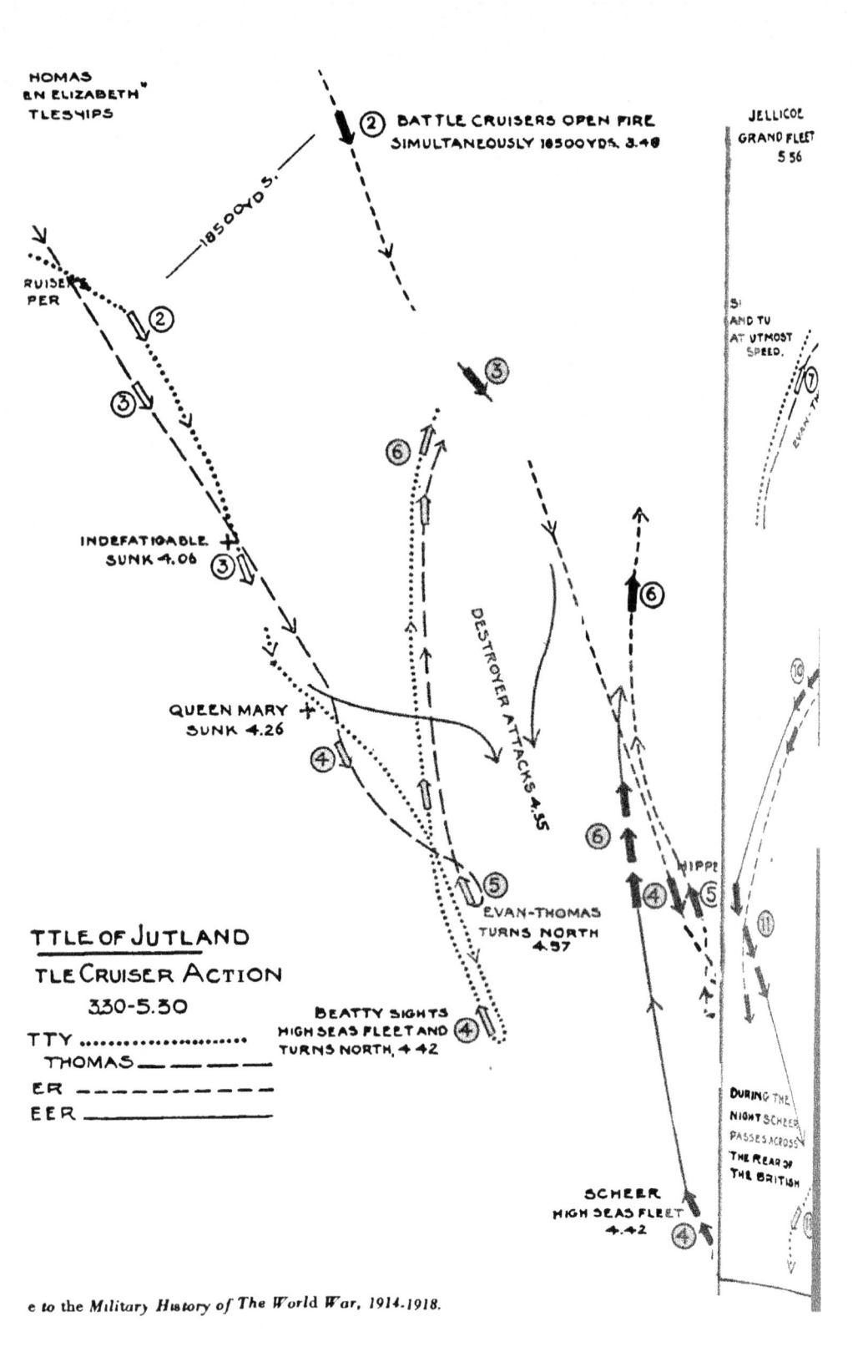

[Map: Battle of Jutland — Battle Cruiser Action 3.30–5.30]

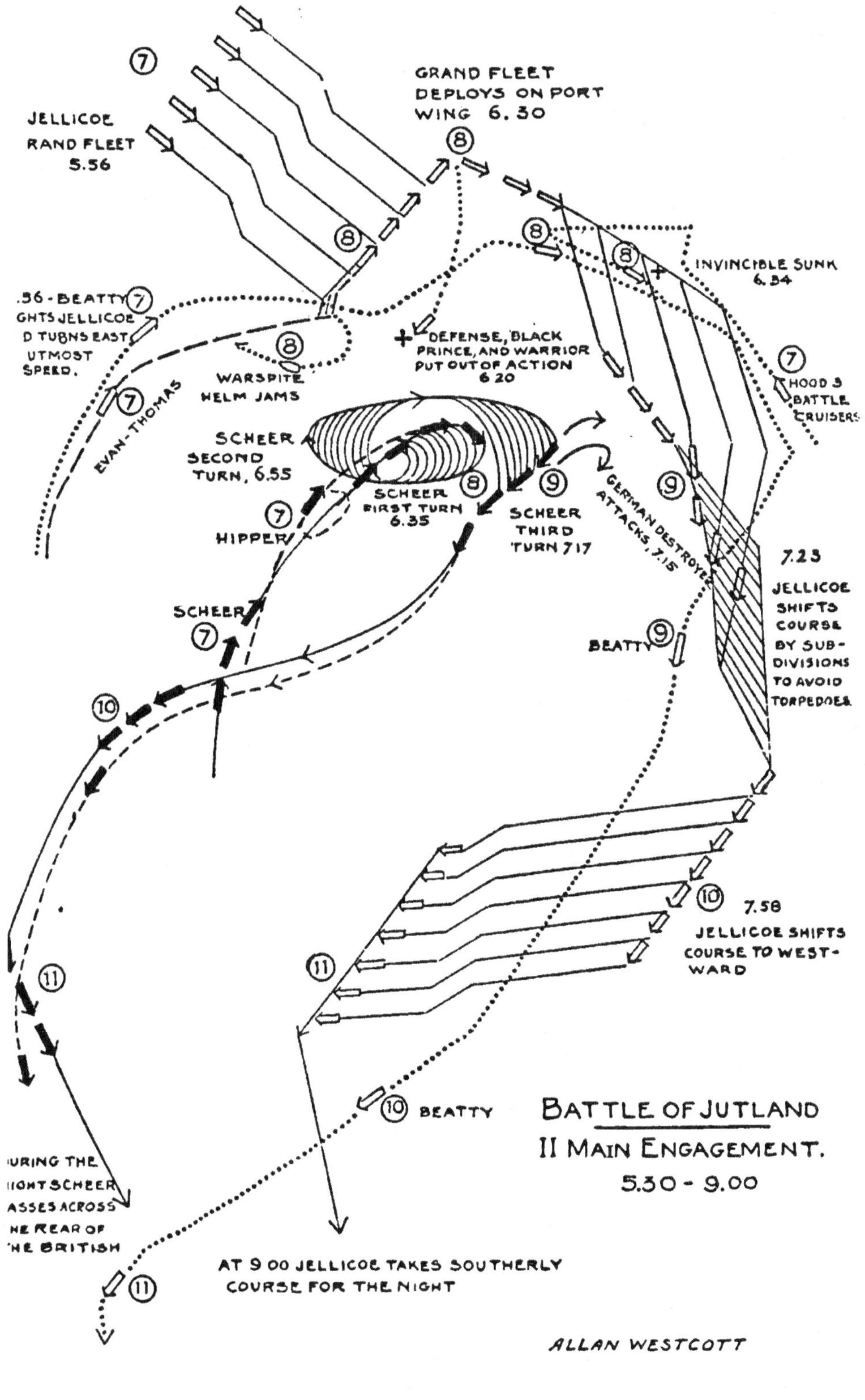

BATTLE OF JUTLAND
II MAIN ENGAGEMENT.
5.30 - 9.00

ALLAN WESTCOTT